SUPER SPORTS STAR KOBE BRYANT

Stew Thornley

Enslow Publishers, Inc.

40 Industrial Road   PO Box 38
Box 398   Aldershot
Berkeley Heights, NJ 07922 Hants GU12 6BP
USA   UK

http://www.enslow.com

Library of Congress Cataloging-in-Publication Data

Thornley, Stew.
    Super sports star Kobe Bryant / Stew Thornley.
        p. cm. — (Super sports star)
Includes bibliographical references and index.
Summary: Profiles the Los Angeles Lakers basketball player, discussing his childhood in Philadelphia, his decision to skip college, and his success with the Lakers.
    ISBN 0-7660-1514-9
 1. Bryant, Kobe, 1978—Juvenile literature. 2. Basketball players—United States—Biography—Juvenile literature. 3. Los Angeles Lakers (Basketball team)—Juvenile literature. [1. Bryant, Kobe, 1978– . 2. Basketball players. 3. Afro-Americans—Biography.] I. Title. II. Series.
    GV884.B794 T56   2001
    796.323'092—dc21
    [B]   00-009119

Printed in the United States of America

10 9 8 7 6 5 4 3 2 1

To Our Readers:
All Internet Addresses in this book were active and appropriate when we went to press. Any comments or suggestions can be sent by e-mail to Comments@enslow.com or to the address on the back cover.

Photo Credits: Andrew D. Bernstein/NBA Photos, pp. 1, 6, 8, 12, 15, 17, 31, 32, 38, 41, 43, 45; Nathaniel S. Butler/NBA Photos, p. 46; Noren Trotman/NBA Photos, p. 36; Rocky Widner/NBA Photos, p. 19; Sam Forencich/NBA Photos, p. 34; Scott Cunningham/NBA Photos, p. 4.

Cover Photo: Andrew D. Bernstein/NBA Photos

CONTENTS

mary
1095

Kobe Bryant towers over two defenders as he flies through the air.

Introduction

Kobe Bryant plays basketball for the Los Angeles Lakers in the National Basketball Association (NBA). The Lakers have an exciting style of play. For many years, the team has been called "Showtime" because of the exciting moves they "show" on the court.

The Lakers have many great players. One of those players is Shaquille O'Neal, their star center. O'Neal gave Bryant the nickname "Showboat" because Bryant's style on the court is so flashy.

Many fans think Kobe Bryant is the most exciting player in the NBA. He can make an assist with an over-the-shoulder pass. He can dunk the ball behind his head. He can fake out players on defense. He can slash and drive to the basket. And, he can hit jump shots from the outside, a long distance away from the basket.

Kobe Bryant shows that he can dunk the basketball behind his head.

Some fans wear Lakers jerseys with his number 8 on them. When Kobe Bryant scores, they scream "Ko-bee!" Sometimes, even the players on other teams shake their heads in wonder.

One of Bryant's teammates once kidded him about his style. Byron Scott said Bryant has to do everything in a dazzling way. "Instead of a plain lay-up," Scott said, "he has to make it spectacular." But Bryant says, "I'm not trying to be flashy. I just do what comes naturally." For Bryant, being flashy comes naturally.

Dazzling Dunks

It was All-Star weekend in 1997. The best players from all the different teams in the NBA got ready to play against each other. The day before the All-Star Game, there were other events. One was the Rookie Game. The top rookies—first-year players—in the league had the chance to show off their best moves. One of those rookies was Kobe Bryant the star guard for the Los Angeles Lakers.

Everyone in the game was in his first year in the NBA, but Bryant was younger than most of them. He had gone straight from high school into the NBA. He never went to college like most of the other players. Bryant was only eighteen years old.

In the Rookie Game, Bryant came out shooting. He took twelve shots in the first half, and had 13 points by halftime. In the second half, Bryant started driving to the basket. He got fouled a lot, and he shot 13 free throws. He made 12 of them.

He finished the game with 31 points. He

had the most points ever scored in a Rookie Game. He also had 8 rebounds. It was a great game, but Bryant had more to do.

Next was the slam-dunk championship. This was open to all the players, not just rookies.

Bryant does not plan his dunks. He does not even decide what he is going to do until he is in the air. "I use my instincts on the way up to the rim." Bryant's first dunk was smooth and powerful. It was good enough for him to make the finals.

In the finals, Bryant charged toward the basket. As he took off, he brought the ball between his legs. Then, he slammed it through the hoop.

He was not done yet. When he landed, he swayed back and forth, and flexed the muscles in his arms. It was all part of the show. Everyone loved it, including the other players on the court.

Bryant's dunk was almost perfect. It earned

him 49 points out of a possible total of 50 points, and he won the slam-dunk championship. He was thrilled. "That's something I've always dreamed about doing since I was a little kid," he said. Now he was playing with the big kids. And he was doing just fine.

Learning the Game

Kobe Bryant was born on August 23, 1978, in Philadelphia, Pennsylvania. He quickly became a basketball fan. Kobe's dad, Joe Bryant, had played in the National Basketball Association (NBA). He was a forward for the Philadelphia 76ers in the 1970s. He later played for the San Diego Clippers and Houston Rockets, before leaving the NBA in 1983. Joe Bryant's nickname was "Jelly Bean," like the candy.

Pam Bryant set up a small basketball court behind their home. That way, Kobe could copy what his dad did. When he was three years old, Kobe began dreaming of someday playing in the NBA.

When Joe Bryant stopped playing in the NBA in 1983, he then played in a league in Italy. His family went with him. It was a great time for Kobe. He visited many different countries in Europe, and he also learned a new language—Italian.

"It was difficult at first because I couldn't

speak Italian," Kobe said. Each day after school, Kobe, Shaya, and Sharia got together. They taught each other the new words they had learned that day. "I was able to speak Italian pretty well within a few months," said Kobe.

As he got older, Kobe learned more about basketball. He learned the basic skills first. "I think most kids who grow up in America learn all the fancy dribbling," Kobe said later. "In Italy, they teach you the true [basics] and leave out all the nonsense."

Of course, Kobe did learn some fancy moves. But he learned the basics first. That process helped him to become a good player. Playing against his dad also helped Kobe to improve. Every summer, the Bryants came back to Philadelphia where Kobe

★ UP CLOSE

Joe and Pam Bryant also had two daughters, Sharia and Shaya. Kobe was the youngest. Joe and Pam Bryant had gone out to a Japanese restaurant before the birth of their son. They saw "Kobe steak" on the menu. They liked the name, so when their son was born, they named him Kobe.

Kobe Bryant learned the basics of good basketball as a small child. He has used what he learned to become the exciting player that he is today.

played in the Sonny Hill League. He struggled at first, but he worked hard and got better.

Jelly Bean Bryant played for eight years in Italy. Then the Bryants moved back to the United States for good in 1991. Kobe was a pretty good player by that time. People were noticing him on the basketball court.

One of the people who noticed Kobe Bryant was Gregg Downer. He was the basketball coach at Lower Merion High School. Coach Downer knew Kobe Bryant was going to be a great player.

A Basketball
Ace

When Kobe Bryant was fourteen years old, he tried something new. He tried dunking the basketball, but it did not turn out very well. "I could barely touch the rim," Kobe said. "It really wasn't a dunk. It was one of those things where you grab the rim and the ball happens to go in. But after that I was really excited. I was really hyped up and dunking was something I worked on."

A lot of things that Kobe tried were hard at first, but he did not quit. He kept trying until he was able to do those things well. Kobe grew a lot in high school. He got to be six feet six inches tall. With his great leaping ability, Kobe was soon able to dunk. He could also pass, shoot, dribble, and rebound really well.

Kobe Bryant became a star on the Lower Merion High School basketball team. In his third year in high school, when he was a junior, Kobe scored an average of 31.1 points per game. He also averaged 10.4 rebounds and 5.2 assists. The Lower Merion Aces made it to the state

Bryant's position on the court is guard. A guard has to be able to shoot from a long distance away from the basket. Kobe Bryant takes aim at the basket.

tournament with Kobe Bryant leading the team.

Kobe's position on the court was point guard. That is the player who directs the team's offense. He calls the plays. A point guard also has to be able to shoot from the outside, a long distance away from the basket. More important, he has able to dribble and pass the ball well. Kobe was able to do all of these things.

He played against good players during the school year. He played against even better players during the summer. He hung out at the gym at St. Joseph's University in Philadelphia. This is where a lot of the players from the Philadelphia 76ers worked out in the summer. Other NBA players who lived near there also came to that gym.

The players let Kobe join them. Rick Mahorn was one of the NBA players who worked out at St. Joseph's. "He blended in with the rest of us," Mahorn said of Bryant. "If you can blend with us as a high school player, that says something right there. It says you belong."

Kobe even tried to dunk the ball on Mahorn once. He did not make it, but Mahorn said, "That's not the point. He actually tried." Kobe said, "I felt real comfortable all summer with the guys. I had no butterflies, no nothing. [I] never felt intimidated. I could get to the hole [basket]. I could hit the jumper. After a while it kind of popped into my mind that I can play with these guys."

When he started his final year of high school in 1995, Kobe was the best high school player in the country. The Lower Merion Aces were not expected to be as good that year as they had been the year before, however. Some of the better players had graduated, but the team still had Bryant. Early in the season, Lower Merion played Philadelphia Roman Catholic, a team with some very good players. Early in the game, Kobe passed the ball a lot. He set up teammates for easy shots. In the second half, though, Kobe started shooting. He scored on eight straight trips to the basket. Roman Catholic tried double-teaming Bryant, assigning two players to defend him. They even triple-teamed him, with three players defending him. But Bryant kept scoring.

Bryant averaged 31 points per game again during his final year at school. And the Lower Merion Aces won the state championship that year.

Bryant also set a new Southeastern Pennsylvania record for most points in a high school career. One player's record that Kobe beat was Wilt Chamberlain's. Chamberlain had played at Overbrook High School in Philadelphia in the 1950s. He later went on to become a great player in the NBA.

A lot of great players go to college after high school. Kobe could have been a star on any college team in the country. He could also have done well with his studies. He was a good student at Lower Merion High School. But he had always wanted to play in the NBA, and he did not want to wait.

In May 1996 he spoke to the students at Lower Merion High School. "I have decided to skip college and take my talents to the NBA. I know I'll have to work extra hard, and I know this is a big step, but I can do it. It's the [chance] of a lifetime. It's time to seize it while I'm young. . . ."

Few players have gone directly from high school into the NBA. Kevin Garnett had done it the year before Bryant did. And Garnett did well in his first season with the Minnesota Timberwolves. But many people wondered if Kobe Bryant would do as well. Some people thought Bryant was making a mistake.

Bryant replied, "I've heard a lot of people say I don't have the maturity yet for the NBA. Well, I've seen things in my lifetime that ordinary kids my age haven't seen or experienced. I've been all through Europe, to France, Germany, lived in Italy, been around

In May 1996, Kobe Bryant announced that he would not be going to college. Instead, he would go straight from high school to the NBA.

professional basketball players my whole life. Growing up the way I have, I think I've matured faster than the ordinary person my age."

Tom McGovern was one of the people who agreed with Bryant's decision. McGovern was the athletic director at Lower Merion High School. He said of Bryant, "In the last four years he's brought us joy, happiness, national recognition—and a state title. We will be behind him 100 percent. We owe him that much."

Breaking In

The Charlotte Hornets picked Kobe Bryant in the first round of the 1996 NBA draft. The draft is how NBA teams choose new players each year. Bryant never played for Charlotte, though. Two weeks after the draft took place, the Hornets traded him to the Los Angeles Lakers.

Bryant played in his first game as a member of an NBA team in early November 1996. He was barely two months past his eighteenth birthday. The Lakers knew Bryant had a lot to learn. They did not expect him to be great right away. Bryant spent a lot of time sitting on the sideline, watching and learning, but he also got his chances on the court.

He had been a point guard in high school, and he sometimes played that position with the

Kobe Bryant fights his way past two defenders on his way to the basket.

Lakers. But he could also play at the other guard spot, known as the shooting guard. Or he could play at the small forward position, if he was needed there.

Bryant got a chance to play a lot in a game in early January 1997. Shaquille O'Neal had hurt his ankle and could not play. Before the game he told Bryant, "you know what you can do. Go do it, and do it under control."

Bryant played well in that game. He had one dunk that he made after turning completely around on his way up to the basket. He made an even better shot late in that game. The Lakers lead over the Sacramento Kings was only four points. Los Angeles had the ball, but the shot clock was running out. The shot clock allows only 24 seconds for a player to shoot the ball at the basket. Nick Van Exel of the Lakers threw up a shot. It was off the mark. Bryant swooped in. He grabbed the ball in the air with his back to the basket. He used both hands to tap it in.

A few weeks later, Bryant was in the

starting lineup of his first professional game. He had 12 points in a 102–83 win over the Dallas Mavericks. He played good defense, too. He guarded Jim Jackson and held the Mavericks' star to 10 points.

In February, Bryant played against Michael Jordan in a game between the Lakers and the Chicago Bulls. The Lakers beat Chicago by sixteen points. One of the exciting moments came when Bryant blocked one of Jordan's shots.

After the game, Bryant said, "I was about 6 when Jordan came into the league. But I won't back down. My attitude is, you can play basketball, but I can play a little, too."

Moving Up

Kobe Bryant had another good game against the Chicago Bulls in his second season. That game was in December 1997, and Bryant scored 33 points.

Bryant was getting more playing time and scoring more points. But he still was not starting in many games. Bryant filled the role of the sixth man, the first player to come off the bench and enter the game as a substitute. It helps if the sixth man can play more than one position. That was the case with Bryant. When he got the chance, he could be explosive. In a game against Houston, he scored 27 points in less than thirteen minutes.

Bryant shows his trademark shot, dunking the ball from behind his head.

Eight times during the season he scored at least 25 points.

Bryant did start in the NBA All-Star Game in February 1998. The fans vote for players in the starting lineup, and the fans wanted Bryant.

Bryant played for the West team. Starting for the East was Michael Jordan. Bryant and Jordan guarded each other. It was a great matchup.

Bryant was nervous before the game. But as soon as the game started, he felt fine. The first time he got the ball, he headed for the hoop. Jordan was in his way, but that did not stop Bryant. He kept going. "Had to," said Bryant, "or he would have killed me."

In the first half, Bryant hit a couple of jump shots over Jordan. A minute later, Bryant got the ball again. He started down court, dribbling behind his back. He broke loose from the pack and headed for the basket all alone. He spun around as he went up and slammed the ball

Kobe Bryant's outstretched arm reaches for the score as he leaps toward the basket.

through the net. It was a 360-degree dunk, and the crowd went wild.

Bryant kept it up in the second half. He made a running hook shot and later drilled a twenty-seven-footer that was good for a three-point basket. At the end of the third quarter, Bryant had 18 points and 6 rebounds. Jordan had 17 points.

Fans wanted to see the battle continue. But Coach George Karl took Bryant out, and he spent the rest of the game on the bench. Jordan kept playing and was voted the game's Most Valuable Player.

For Bryant, it was a great game. Playing against Jordan helped him learn a lot. "I can use it for my knowledge in the future," Bryant said. It was the last All-Star Game for Michael Jordan, who retired at the end of the season.

One superstar was on his way out, but another was on his way up.

Making the Grade

Kobe Bryant was ready for his third season in the NBA. He would have to wait, though. The 1998–99 season did not start on time. There was a dispute between the players and the owners, and the first part of the season was cancelled. Games did not begin until February 1999.

Bryant started in the Lakers' first game against the Houston Rockets. Early in the game, he took a pass from Shaquille O'Neal and made a reverse lay-up. It was a good start.

Bryant guarded Scottie Pippen in the game. Pippen scored only 10 points. Meanwhile, Bryant had 25 points and 10 rebounds. That was the most rebounds he ever had in a game.

Bryant started every one of the Lakers' games during the season. He was still young, but the Lakers thought he could do the job. He gave them good reasons to feel that way.

In March, the Lakers were having trouble against the Orlando Magic. The Magic led by 24 points at one time. But then Kobe Bryant took

Kobe Bryant goes up for the score as two defenders from the Houston Rockets look on.

over, and showed all his moves. He made every shot he took in the third quarter. He stayed hot in the final period. He scored a total of 33 points in the second half, helping the Lakers to win the game.

The Lakers made the playoffs. Their first opponent was Houston, and the Lakers won the playoff series. In the final game, Bryant had 24 points, 8 assists, 6 rebounds, 3 steals, and 2 blocks.

He had more good games in the next series, but the Lakers lost to the San Antonio Spurs. The Spurs went on to win the NBA title.

The Lakers' season was over. But the team and Kobe Bryant had made progress. The Lakers and Kobe Bryant made it all the way to the Finals against the Indiana Pacers in 2000. Bryant hurt his ankle

UP CLOSE

Bryant helps people learn to read and write. Some people still have trouble with that, even after they become adults. Bryant also set up the Kobe Bryant Scholarship to help young people pay for college.

during the series, but he came back. The Lakers won the series in six games to gain their first championship title since 1988. Kobe Bryant and Shaquille O'Neal led the Lakers to victory.

Kobe Bryant has his own house in California. Bryant's parents live with him. Joe Bryant had been an assistant basketball coach at La Salle University in Philadelphia. When Kobe went into the NBA, his father quit his coaching job. He now manages his son's career.

Joe and Pam Bryant raised their son to be an individual. Kobe Bryant does things his way. He has no tattoos or earrings. Bryant said, "the key to success at anything, I think, is avoiding peer pressure."

UP CLOSE

Bryant's favorite athlete is football player Emmitt Smith of the Dallas Cowboys. "He plays with a lot of desire," Bryant said. "He works hard and he's a great person. I also admire all-time home-run champ Hank Aaron [baseball player]."

Bryant's favorite cartoon character is "the Road Runner because he can't be caught." The same can be said of Kobe Bryant.

Bryant went straight from high school to the NBA. But he takes classes at the University of California at Los Angeles (UCLA). He is studying international business.

Moves like this one brought Kobe Bryant and the Lakers to the Finals against the Indiana Pacers in 2000.

CAREER STATISTICS

				NBA						
Team	**Year**	**GP**	**FG%**	**FT%**	**REB**	**AST**	**STL**	**BLK**	**PTS**	**PPG**
Lakers	1996–97	71	.417	.889	132	91	49	23	539	7.6
Lakers	1997–98	79	.428	.794	242	199	74	40	1,220	15.4
Lakers	1998–99	50	.465	.839	264	190	72	50	996	19.9
Lakers	1999–2000	66	.468	.821	416	323	106	62	1,485	22.5
Totals		**266**	**.450**	**.816**	**1,054**	**803**	**301**	**175**	**4,240**	**15.9**

GP—Games Played   **REB**—Rebounds   **BLK**—Blocked Shots
FG%—Field Goal Percentage   **AST**—Assists   **PTS**—Points
FT%—Free Throw Percentage   **STL**—Steals   **PPG**—Points Per Game

Where to Write to Kobe Bryant

Mr. Kobe Bryant
Los Angeles Lakers
Staples Center
1111 S. Figueroa St.
Los Angeles, CA 90015

Kobe Bryant leaps and aims for the basket.

WORDS TO KNOW

assist—A pass to a teammate who makes a basket.

bank shot—A shot that bounces (or banks) off the backboard.

baseline—The out-of-bounds line that runs behind the basket.

dishing off—Passing to a teammate.

double-teaming—Two defenders guarding one player.

draft—The way NBA teams choose new players each year.

dunk—A shot that is slammed through the basket from directly above the basket. Also known as a slam or slam dunk.

fadeaway—A shot taken while falling away from the basket.

jump hook—A one-handed shot taken while jumping.

outside shot—A shot taken a long distance away from the basket.

rebound—Getting the basketball after a missed shot.

Kobe Bryant is sandwiched between two defenders as he goes up for the shot.

shot clock—A clock that limits the amount of time to shoot the ball. The shot clock in the NBA is twenty-four seconds.

triple-teaming—Three defenders guarding one player.

turnaround—A shot taken after the player has turned to face the basket.

Bryant shows his intensity as he goes up for the shot.

46

READING ABOUT

Books

Kirkpatrick, Rob. *Kobe Bryant: "Slam Dunk" Champion*. Minneapolis, Minn.: The Rosen Publishing Group, Inc., 1999.

Schrackenberg, Robert E. *Kobe Bryant*. Broomall, Pa.: Chelsea House Publishers, 1999.

Stewart, Mark. *Kobe Bryant: Hard to the Hoop*. Missoula, Mont.: Mountain Press Publishing Co., Inc., 2000.

"10 Questions for Kobe Bryant," *Sports Illustrated for Kids*, October 1997, p. 28.

Internet Addresses

The Official Web Site of the NBA
<http://www.nba.com/playerfile/kobe_bryant.html>

The Official Web Site of the Lakers
<http://www.nba.com/lakers>

INDEX